Tactful
Advice
for Calling Your
Next
Pastor

Gary Straub

CBP®

ST. LOUIS, MISSOURI

Cover design: Jesse Turri

CBPBooks.com

Print: 9780827237124
EPUB: 9780827237131   EPDF: 9780827237148

Printed in the United States of America

Contents

Dedication

Special thanks to Bethany Fellows, a ministry that serves congregations by assisting newly ordained ministers in the transition from seminary to full-time parish work with a healthy sense of pastoral identity. This coaching, mentoring, and prayerful ministry was originally founded on a grant from The Lilly Endowment, who graciously extended two additional grants, creating a fifteen-year window of experience in the care and calling of young "first-time" ministers. I have been blessed by the opportunity to listen to both sides of the conversation around "A Call." Often the invitation is initiated by congregational leaders willing to work with freshly ordained ministers in transition to congregational life. I am also blessed to be privy to the continual conversation with young pastors as they weigh early professional decisions which help set the course of their careers as they follow this intriguing and confounding mystery we call "A Call."

As the work of Bethany Fellows now extends ecumenically to other mainline faith communities, the invitation into conversation with congregational leaders, middle judicatories, and seminaries continues to enrich the dialogue and deepen our learnings.

This book is a collection of practical field observations I can really only call advice. If something you read here works for you, Alleluia!

If it proves spectacularly unhelpful... Well, keep on looking!

Your persistence in this task of calling ministers is too critical not to seek all the help you can get!

Gary Straub, Louisville, Kentucky, All Saints' Day – 2015

Introduction

It probably shouldn't have surprised me to Google around a bit and discover the emergence of an entrepreneurial edge to the time-honored task of calling ministers to local congregations. Although Jesus did not form a search team when he called Peter and John out of their family fishing boats to a lifetime of ministry, things do change.

A barnstorming tour of church history highlights the morphing of the call process since New Testament times. Early church bishops "made the calls" with apostolic authority. When kings and bishops began vying for the power of appointment, the calling process became more efficient, if somewhat tainted. Amidst post-Reformation churches, the calling of a local shepherd became a fiercely guarded right. However, making the "right" call proved elusive on occasion. Later, as denominations formed, judicatory officials assumed the mantle and created systems and processes, which have clarified some things and clouded others.

At the far edge of our post-denominational era, a virtual cottage industry has emerged as an alternative to the standard mainline search/call approach. A niche market is arising in the space just beyond the current systems. While present methods assist in vetting character, assessing skill levels, and tracking records of effectiveness; the match of hopes, dreams, temperaments, and gifts can prove elusive for both ministers and congregations.

Unless a minister has a mentor, the learning curve around calling is steep; and the level of "human resources" expertise in most local congregations is thin. While general guidelines are available, the requirements of today's workplace call for legal and technical knowledge beyond the scope of most congregational leaders seeking a pastor. In this gap, independent online church search firms are advertising hired counsel, making attractive claims, offering guarantees, and boasting some spectacular results. In my own mind, the jury is still out on these "holy hiring" trends, where the science of recruiting leaders is increasingly applied to the ancient art of calling a pastor.

My hope, however, is that the intersection of conversation with industry hiring methods, independent headhunting techniques, present denominational systems, and the old grapevine will yield fresh fruit for both the callers and the called.

No matter who makes the call and by whatever preferred means, good calls, like marriages, are still made in heaven.

A Few Words on
Ministerial Farewells

A change of ministers places strain and stress on a congregation. No matter the circumstances, a pastoral vacancy creates a spiritual crisis for which most congregations are unprepared.

We often respond with attempts to keep the church activity calendar full. While preserving the regular rhythms of congregational life is important, the most critical need is to declare a season of community reflection on core identity, mission, vision, and values. Looking in the mirror is tough work; it's easy to see why congregations facing a pastoral leadership transition default to the more practical starting points—such as organizing the task of finding an interim and appointing a search team, gaining assistance from denominational leaders, shoring up finances, and tackling maintenance issues as a way of expressing unanimity. Our collective anxiety presses for a quick resolution on a short timeline. The "to do" list is daunting, but not nearly as daunting as the deeper matters: grief work, sober evaluation of our collective effectiveness, prayer around our core reasons for being, attending matters of the heart around communal healing and reconciliation, and authentic soul conversation about what we need to be and to be about—for the sake of the gospel and the world around us.

Underlying these tasks are the emotional dynamics of grief and loss, which are often unacknowledged, and therefore unowned and operating dynamically on a *sub rosa* level. The odd quirks, emotional outbursts, and near-fanatical focus on relatively trivial pursuits might catch one off guard, if not understood as being grief-related.

A word around farewells: Saying our farewell thoroughly and with integrity gives expression to the heart and soul of a congregation. Good "goodbyes" set the stage for healthy "hellos." The portrait of your congregation's most recent farewell may not have been painted by Norman Rockwell. Farewells need not be picture perfect, but they need to come from a heartfelt, healthy place and remain a blessing in the congregation's memory. In choreographing our goodbyes, let courteous compromise and gracious accommodation prevail. A congregational leader who is alert to the underlying dynamics can help preserve the goodness of community memory.

Frankly, not every goodbye can be a good one. The dark side of congregational life sometimes seeps out during transitions. There are the hard realities of betrayal, broken trust, unbecoming conduct, and uncharitable behavior on the congregation's part...and then there is also the minister's conduct to consider. Church life can turn ugly in a heartbeat, and my advice only echoes the apostle Paul's congregational counsel in Romans 12:18: "so far as it depends on you, live peaceably with all." Admittedly, Paul's peaceable stance is rooted more deeply at some times than at other times. That said, there is wisdom in taking the high road during rough partings. If nothing else, your next minister is taking mental notes on how you handle difficult and unpleasant matters.

Congregational behaviors exhibiting passive aggressiveness, gossip, and conflict avoidance while lobbing pot shots from a safe emotional distance are not top vote-getters among ministers considering a new call. Whatever the circumstance and assessment of blame, nasty farewells often reveal unresolved congregational conflict and undermine the character of the community. Attitudes exhibited during a church transition may expose bullying or acting out behavior that might otherwise have remained hidden. As a member of the Search Team, these incidents tell you what you need to know in describing the congregation's quirks to a potential candidate. Take note of personalities that disrupt or at least disturb the peace of the fellowship. Interventions may be necessary. These are clearly distractions to a good goodbye.

After we have said our farewells and made good our goodbyes, it's time to press on with the process, right? Because the church is made up of human beings, politics are unavoidable and questions arise. How do we sustain spiritual momentum and mission focus in what feels like a leadership vacuum? How do we maintain equilibrium in balance of power issues yet keep momentum strong?

How do we avoid the encroachment of long-established power cliques but engage their support for the future? How do we speak to legitimate concerns and avoid giving old gripes a grip? That giant sucking sound sometimes heard in board meetings could be the power vacuum working overtime to reconstitute the congregation just like it was in 1958, which was a great year; it's just not next year.

Many members who sit on the sidelines as careful observers of the search process will be looking for evidence of congregational well-being. The most tangible, standard yardsticks are offerings and attendance. In my experience, the majority of churches in transition experience a drop in both. There certainly are exceptions, but don't be shocked if the numbers trend downward slightly (15 to 20 percent). On the up side, we can find additional ways to measure morale. For instance, are new leaders emerging out of the pews to bridge the gap, help steady the ship, and guide the process? Do people hang around for a bit of fellowship after the meeting work is done? What does the buzz in the room tell you? Who are the quiet caregivers who minister in the background and step into the foreground in the minister's absence? Are there new people speaking up and offering positive initiatives? Who exhibits some skill in helping to stabilize church operations and strengthen mission while we prepare to launch a critical decision process that will impact the years ahead? Who are your 'gap minders'? Identify them, call them out of the woodwork, engage and companion them in these odd, in-between moments.

Help is available for congregations in search of a minister. Most denominations or church bodies have middle judicatory leaders who can be of great assistance. Likely there is an established manual of procedures available and a visit scheduled with your search team. The emphasis is necessarily on steps and check lists—all of which can be quite helpful. That said, the internal dynamics and the spiritual dimensions of the process might not always receive the focused attention required for an effective search. The aim of this book is to integrate practical advice with prayerful counsel.

With pastoral tenures shorter than ever and mainline congregations experiencing massive shifts in church culture as well as internal ripple effects of grief and loss, finding a new minister is a complex process to manage. "Manage" is the metaphor of choice. Understandably, a congregation going through a leadership transition frequently tightens its belt and operates more intentionally out of a business model. With so many moving parts in flux, following the time-tested steps of an orderly procedure can be comforting. Attending to "the good of the order" can translate as an expression of care for the congregation. When folks in the pews begin to notice congregational leaders are paying attention to procedural detail and working the process, it feels like the lights are still on and someone who cares is minding the store.

All to the good; but there is more. And this "more" falls mostly in the category of advice. I write out of a desire to distill and convey fifty years of pastoral experience: three calls to large congregations, followed by eight interim ministry positions and countless hours in coaching conversation with both the candidates as well as with the chairs of search teams. My aim is to articulate the dynamics of the search process from both sides of the conversation. I hope something you read now might resonate at a later time, perhaps when your process seems to bog down. Maybe an insight gleaned here helps move your deliberations off dead center. But in all things, keep talking to each other. Healthy dialogue helps keep you fiercely open to the Holy Spirit. To me, this is a critical core value for an effective search team. Staying open is not just a matter of proper procedure, it is also paying prayerful attention to what John calls "what the Spirit is saying to the churches." (Rev. 2:29) . Are you listening with the ears of the heart?

Your team is charged with a high honor, and is committing to a serious investment of time. The calling of a minister is an admittedly daunting task. (It is no less daunting and humbling to be the one being called!)

One search team chair described it as similar to the process of making steel. "Imagine hot molten metal: poured, cooled, rolled, and extruded into useful parts. Our committee feels the strain of being heated and cooled, stretched, hammered, and finally extruded into odd shapes that are eventually molded into working parts!" Another search chair said, "This search process is a whole other world—kinda like Alice in Wonderland, falling down a rabbit hole into an alternative universe!" Both comments allude to ways the search process opens dimensions that are not normally part of the weekly church life most of us encounter. It is an odd, "out of time" sort of time: less *chronos* (clock) time and more *kairos* time (moments of God's appointment). Leading a search process or participating as a team member opens us to a communion of spirits: human and holy. It is indeed a kairos kind of time: a season not measured in minutes, but movements of the Spirit among us. I invite you to welcome and savor these moments. They are rare and precious gifts.

Brass Tacks/Tacts

In the wild west of Texas in the '60s, (that's the 1860s) a slang phrase became common parlance: "Getting down to brass tacks." In the general store's haberdashery section, cloth was measured by stretching the bolt from nose to fingertip and calling it a yard. Close enough? Imagine how a clerk with short arms might save a proprietor innumerable yards of valuable inventory over a year's time. Customers felt short-changed. A new standard was introduced: two brass tacks exactly 36 inches apart, nailed into the edge of the fabric counter. Customer satisfaction soared.

When it comes to the contemporary search for a minister, most of the old-time haberdashery methods have been eliminated. Finding a minister has been measured, studied, routinized, and computerized. Denominational offices crank out e-reams of profiles and resumes. Search teams are charged with the task of describing, measuring, and profiling their congregations in numerical terms. There are moments of feeling both inundated and underwhelmed with data. However daunting the technology may be, it does take some of the "by guess and by golly" factor out of the process. Some of the next steps include candidate ranking by selective criteria, Skype interviews, and site visits. Before you know it, the search team's chairperson will be negotiating the terms of call with a successful candidate...right?

Here's where the "brass tacts" image comes into play. When it's time to close the deal, brass tacts require a velvet-gloved hammer to nail down the particulars of firming the financial arrangements and confirming the call. This means more than employing shrewd negotiating tactics to seal a deal. Let's back up and have a look at the whole congregational journey—from the grief of losing a minister to the delight of welcoming a new pastoral leader.

When your present pastor announces plans to leave, a new set of congregational dynamics comes into play. Shock and grief often dominate the atmosphere. Some folks express intense feelings while others withdraw to the sidelines with a wait-and-see attitude. Almost always, a few folks leave the congregation. This panics the leadership, but it is fairly normal for people to 'get on and off the bus' during congregational transitions. While the reasons are myriad, the rhythms are predictable. Therefore, writing an appropriate ending to the church's present ministry chapter and setting the stage for a healthy search process means finding ways to say a good 'good bye,' not only to the departing pastor but to a few members as well.

While the period between the initial announcement and the final farewell may seem interminable, this intervening season can become a rich time of taking stock, as the sense of ownership shifts from pastor to rest more heavily on the shoulders of the current congregational leaders. It is not uncommon for the Search Team to be unconsciously inclined to find someone much like the beloved pastor who is leaving. Or, if the departure is messy, the accent shifts to making sure the next pastor will "not turn out to be just like the last one." One of the reasons search teams receive the advice to take their time and not rush precipitously into a new call is that there is a certain amount of psychic space any pastor occupies by reason of the office. It requires a reasonable amount of time to take a deep breath, step back, assess your situation, and broaden your perspective. Do this! Don't be rushed by someone who has a hot prospect that is going to get away if the search team won't hurry. Proceed at the pace of a passionate mosey.

In this intervening time, a congregation's DNA emerges. Some churches are strongly "pastor-led," while others operate with more of a collaborative ministry partnership style. So don't get railroaded into a quick-fix mentality. Leadership transitions provide occasion and sacred space to re-examine, explore, and adjust leadership style, and to do a full audit and review of the big picture dynamics.

During this review, leaders become aware that the loyalty previously expressed through faith in the pastor is now to be directed more fully toward God.

The ultimate stewardship for the congregation and accountability for mission rests heavily on the elected leaders (and informal wisdom leaders) until a new ministerial partnership can be established. Being a church officer, board member, elder, deacon, trustee, or ministry leader during times of transition can be a larger-than-life challenge. With the official resignation/ retirement/leaving letter, the whole congregation begins referring to the present in the past tense, and moves into "previous pastor zone." With the help of a skilled interim, this odd interlude can be devoted to analyzing capacities and future needs while fulfilling pastoral and administrative responsibilities.

So, the immediate concern is securing pulpit supply and/or selecting an interim minister. Most denominations have their own process and procedures. Please don't set up unrealistic hopes and expectations for this in-between season. Make sure your entire congregation goes to school on the basic tasks of the interim transition.

Interims as Sherpas

The world's highest mountain peaks would not be climbed successfully without the work of Sherpa guides. Interim ministers enjoy a rare privilege to serve as Sherpa's—trail guides through the thickets of the spiritual leadership transition. There are icy paths to avoid, tricky crevasses to cross, heavy burdens to shoulder, logistics to plot, wisdom around weather, critical crampons to place that anchor dangerous passages, and short-cuts. Sherpas don't cost; they pay!

The first task for an interim minister is learning to say a healthy hello and grace-filled goodbye so that interim dynamics do not add drama to the congregation's already overloaded emotional circuits. This calls for a low-maintenance ego; good interim ministers know it's "not *your* church" and it's also "not *their* church," either; it's Christ's church. Interim ministers should understand the underlying dynamics of ownership. Look for a healthy attitude that says: "This interim call is *not* all about me." Gaining clarity around the practical implications of this claim is critical to startup because the sense of congregational ownership is deeply disturbed during pastoral transitions. This doesn't mean an interim minister can't inject his or her personality and make a powerful impact. It simply means that the ego is crucified with Christ, and directed by the deeper energies through a calm personality full of prayerful integrity. Spiritually, this calls for someone who lives with a measure of mature wisdom and operates comfortably out of his or her experience of the heart of God.

The interim minister's work can be summarized as fourfold:

1. Interims recover, review, redefine, and refocus the mission and purpose of the congregation, moving forward. This involves simple things: from identifying and solving problems, to more complex matters, such as managing appropriate change. It can be anything from tweaking procedures to addressing deeper systemic issues. Expect some astonishing revelations and defining moments along this path. Think of this time as a wilderness journey, analogous to the Old Testament stories of God's children wandering in wilderness, led by Moses. (*Note:* interims should *not* last 40 years.)

2. Interims focus primary energy on staff and leadership circles to address immediate issues and opportunities. It is not at all unusual for matters previously avoided to surface. Unaddressed, they become energy drains. However painful, patterns around conflict dynamics need clear identification and fullest examination. Helping

leaders recognize core congregational values and DNA also means defining who we are not. Since few congregations have the capacity to be all things to all people, aligning missional energies to match core values requires clarity and integrity. It is a blessed relief to learn what we can realistically accomplish from what we wish were (still) true of our congregation. This work is anguish well worth the effort.

3. Interims serve a low-profile role as in-house consultants, coaches, and spiritual guides to core staff and primary leadership. The capacity to quickly establish trust-filled, safe, confidential working relationships is a must. Let me mention an additional interim grace: a healthy sense of humor. It's a life saver, in many awkward church situations, to enjoy the capacity to laugh with (and not at) one another! Church life can offer the daily adult minimum dose of irony. If you are paying attention and not afraid of a healthy laugh, there is no IRONy deficiency in your congregation.

4. Interims play a kind of "holy spirit" role, coming alongside, companioning, and encouraging greater spiritual depth. They do all of this while enjoying the daily rhythms of congregational life as the primary preaching minister and spiritual leader. Interims play a "John the Baptist" role to "prepare the way for the one

who is to come." During my own tenure as an interim, I recall one woman introducing me to a visitor and explaining, "Now, this is not our *real* minister; this is *just* the interim." I barely possessed the wit to play along: "Yes, and hello there. I am not the real minister; I am only the faux minister. A verified, certified, and authenticated and duly licensed pastor will appear in the pulpit in two weeks. So, y'all come back, hear?"

Beyond the basic, outlined interim tasks, the small print always reads: "...and such duties as may be assigned." Most congregations are astonished at the deluge of tasks that fall by default to the minister and about which the interim (to say nothing of the incoming minister) will have absolutely no clue. Expect some surprises here. Lots of operational procedures are built around personalities and preferences, so now is a great time to review, rework, and reassign.

Transitional Matters

Congregations in transition need foundational stability in anticipation of changes ahead. While rules and procedures are considered a necessary bother by some, the upside is that these rules and procedures can insure orderly transitional guidance and build confidence in the present leadership.

Much as I encourage calculated risks, the better counsel is probably to play by the rules and go by the book. This does not mean you should take whoever comes along as your interim minister. Study up on the requirements, skills, and tasks required of a competent interim. Ask around. You do not want a babysitter or someone who is operating out of a grand sense of yesteryear. What are the congregation's self-identified needs during this season? Can your team articulate your mission in authentic and believable terms? Get some practice. I advise deliberate conversation around these core matters, because all decisions come under intense scrutiny during transitions and need to be measured by DNA, mission, vision, and values. Risks that might be considered in the normal range of probability take on added freight during seasons of congregational stress. Cutting corners and taking hasty short cuts in order to save time invites unnecessary criticism from those who intensely watch from the sidelines for the slightest rule infraction. Don't be controlled by this scrutiny, just be aware that the watchers are watching.

All I'm saying is that the people skills of the congregational leadership team will get a full workout because anxiety runs high and comes into play around decisions made in the transition process. So, give careful attention to detail. Take all the counsel you can, solicit good advice, widen your wisdom circles, and broaden your horizons. This advice applies especially to the process for selecting a search team, which is often spelled out in the congregation's governance. Here are a couple of quick scenarios to illustrate how church by-laws, procedures, protocol, and precedence often operate in the transitional arena:

Fairview Church's by-laws dictate that the search committee for calling an interim minister automatically becomes the permanent search team. However, the by-laws offer no requirements for composition of the team, beyond official membership. While allowing for flexibility, this practice also opened the door to unfair accusations of favoritism or politics. Fairview's structure offered no safe container to hold their grief and anxiety, which "went sideways" and created quirks and quasars—mistrustful blips on the screen. Speculation and gossip were never addressed, and created a sour atmosphere around a sacred task.

Valley Church's prescribed governance for its search team insisted on a strictly democratic approach, with full representation from nearly every sub-group. This approach excluded some key opinion makers who currently held no official title. Think about creative ways to include and involve these leaders. Also, the large team size made decisions unwieldy and ponderous. Valley learned the hard way that the best time to review by-laws and make critical changes and recommendations around search team composition is when you don't need them. Dissent over vague language led to wrangles of interpretation that delayed their process.

Generally speaking, if the previous minister's tenure was fruitful, the search team brims with confidence in launching the work of call. If the previous tenure turned rocky, the search team often begins with more clarity around what they are *not* looking for. The period following search team formation is an excellent time for encouraging a season of congregational conversation and prayer, which the team needs to process together as part of their own team building. Do not skip this stage. Get to know one another at deeper levels, build relational trust, and clarify the tasks at hand before plunging into the official business of search. Find ways to balance the team's interpersonal spiritual process with the official procedures. Taking the time to build team trust and know each other along this journey will influence the outcome more than is apparent on the front end. You will find examples of ways to develop team trust and spiritual agreement in another chapter.

After the interim is selected, *plan a time out to settle into new rhythms.*

Alternate succession plans beyond the tried and true interim approach are possible, but the reason you haven't heard about them is that they aren't often tried. One example is the "ascending associate" model, which requires a high degree of trustful conversation about succession. Most churches find this conversation extremely awkward, like the "elephant in the room." Pursuing this option requires a considerably longer lead time and superlative cooperative spirit from incoming and outgoing ministers, and the leaders who surround both. With so much either/or thinking prevalent in the culture, the "both/and" thinking of this approach calls forth maximum maturity. So most churches go the traditional interim route. But there are brilliant exceptions. Is there anything in your leadership DNA that says this might be worthy of consideration?

After the interim is selected, attention turns to the search team selection process. Be attentive to the spirit and attitude around which this group forms. Foster the kind of transparent, open-hearted, in-depth conversation that yields spiritual agreement. Search teams feeling pressured for quick results may be tempted to neglect or bypass the team molding, shaping, and gelling process. The quality and depth of a search team's spiritual interconnectedness shows up at the interview stage and leaves an impression on interviewees. The kind of candidate you are looking for will be savvy about reading your group dynamics, so invest the time on the front end to discover, explore, and develop relational trust within the team. In the end, it will save time.

These days, search teams will seldom be successful without enlisting cooperation from your middle judicatory. Give attention to this working relationship. The process can go a lot more smoothly with a spirit of mutual respect. Whether you are relating to a conference pastor, district superintendent, or regional minister, building rapport helps. In most church systems, no informational access to the pool of candidates is granted until the congregation does its own analytical homework and can realistically depict their context, mission, style, and staff needs. This means field research and paperwork so your congregation can be profiled and logged into the system. These exercises and the resulting data help your middle judicatory sort through potential candidates and refer to you those who are reasonable potential matches. While this match-up process works well in theory, it may or may not happen in real time. Still, it is in your best interest to give this your best effort. Without orientation to the process and some instruction sessions that judicatory leaders provide, your results may be less than desirable.

As an interim, a church consultant, a coach to young pastors, and an informal advisor to search team leaders, I find transition times to be a key opportunity to strengthen trust between congregations and their denominational affiliation. If your relationship to the wider church is frayed, fractured, or in disrepair, act now to intentionally re-engage. When congregational life is smooth, it is easy to slip into smug stand-offishness, to imagine that we are not joined to the wider body of Christ. However, when pastoral transition occurs, you will need help and cooperation from your denominational leaders. Don't isolate, engage! Begin by giving the benefit of the doubt. Offer and invite a sincere co-operative spirit. A receptive atmosphere creates the context to discover the necessary tools for launching the search process. Please ask for what you need. I trust you will get all the official help you need, and you will need it all.

One further word about the rules: Whatever opinions may prevail within your congregation about how arcane the denominational process is for calling a new minister, no matter how unbalanced/unfair the process seems, no matter how it appears to privilege a certain group or category, no matter how outmoded and creaky the software, no matter how labyrinthian the rules of the game, set your qualms aside. This process may be vastly improved a century from now; but now is your search window. Once you have been properly schooled in the game, play! Working with the system, learning how to navigate, mastering the rules of the road—all of these simply get you to the starting line. You are then granted an official "search-and-call license." The protocols, which may seem pointless and tedious, preserve everybody's options. The hunt is on.

Sidebar: As you begin reading resumes/relocation papers and making inquiries, a word about church manners: let old-fashioned business courtesy prevail. The prompt manner with which you handle callbacks and thank-yous and initiate timely follow-up makes a huge positive impression and creates a lot of good will. Ministerial candidates regularly report that timely responses, prompt callbacks, and common business courtesy are all too uncommon. Thoughtfulness, manners, and timely responses create a positive atmosphere, which fosters an effective call. Don't string candidates along. Let them know frankly and promptly where they stand with you. They have other fish to fry as well. It's a tricky tango, and it takes two, and your courtesy creates positive vibes!

Candid Comments from Candidates

The following are personal observations of young pastors who were recently in the search process. They were asked: "What would you want to encourage search committees to keep in mind as they interview candidates? What did you really like that you experienced? What do you hope to never go through again?" These candid belows remarks offer insight into the internal dynamics of the search process, with the hope that your team will reflect and discuss these comments as excellent preparation for the actual contact and initial interview process.

From a senior minister who is married, the father of two young sons:

1. Communicate the flow of your process with the candidates. The committee might interview one or two candidates a week for four weeks, then deliberate for a few weeks, then have Easter, then get around to calling a candidate back and letting him or her know where things are. In the meantime, you're keeping someone who is considering a major life change (potentially involving his or her family) in the dark about

where he or she stands. Simple things—such as when you're meeting next and a date the candidates can expect to hear something from you; these go a long way! They convey a level of understanding and respect you would also expect a candidate to have.

2. Pay competitively. You are compensating a person with a three-year master's degree—a professional in every sense of the term. No one goes into ministry expecting to get rich, but they do hope they will not pass a financial burden on to their spouses and children because of their vocation. Some churches expect that when one pastor leaves, they can reduce salaries back to the level they were when they called the previous person. It doesn't work that way. And, a dose of reality: ministry is like some other vocations; you get what you pay for.

3. Do not be bound by experience as the sole qualifying factor. In many instances, an experienced pastor may not be what a congregation needs at a given time. A younger person, with less experience, may be uniquely suited for where your church is in its history and able to flex for what is needed for the immediate future. In an ideal world, you want a talented leader with experience—but I would sacrifice experience to get someone who is uniquely gifted.

4.   Be serious about respecting confidentiality in the process. The candidate may not want to go to dinner in a public place with the whole committee for the in-person visit. If he or she is already serving a church, given present commitments the candidate may not be able to communicate with you at particular times or places. Keep in mind that you are working with someone who already has a church—one they would prefer to keep should they not get yours!

From a senior pastor, a single woman

1.   Please examine your hearts (and your congregation) for unspoken expectations. Convert unspoken expectations into spoken ones. For example, I discovered that an unspoken expectation my congregation has for me is to not start a family in the next couple of years. This only became evident in maternal leave negotiations. In relation to this, please consider leading on the leave policy. This means providing generous paid leave (at least 8 weeks) for both mothers and fathers, for birth or adoption. In this area, the church can be a leader for our country (which is woefully behind all other developed countries). Put a generous maternal leave policy in place even if your candidate is unmarried, not of child-bearing age, etc.

2. Skype may be great for the committee, but I found it to be not as helpful for me. It was difficult to see clearly the facial expressions of the committee (because of resolution problems or connection issues). Sometimes I couldn't tell who was speaking. In committee Skype sessions, it was extra-helpful to go around the table slowly with introductions so I write down names and create a chart of where they were sitting. Build a bit of on-line community.

3. Quick and courteous feedback is a must for those candidates you decide to pass on, as well as for those you wish to converse with further. For those you decide to pass on, make sure your e-mail or letter is not just a form letter. Try to make it a tiny bit personal.

4. One thing that really encouraged me to pursue negotiations with the church where I accepted a call was they built Bethany Fellows into the first draft of the letter of call without me having to ask for it. I had listed it (a peer and mentoring group described at BethanyFellows.org) in my papers and they took it seriously. This small act let me know they cared about my own development as a pastor. I would encourage congregations to do something similar—let your incoming pastor know that you care and will actively support his or her health and ongoing spiritual development.

5. Please know that if there are members of the search committee who are tired/cranky/don't want to be there, your candidates will likely pick up on that and it will make them not want to be there either. On the other hand, your search committee members may enjoy being around each other so much that they neglect to watch the time and are overly chatty during the interview. Please try to strike a balance on this.

6. Let your candidate know why you're interested! Flattery feels good, but it also clues the candidate in to what you're looking for/ desiring/expecting. We need to know if you are clear about what you are seeking.

From a senior minister, a woman married with a young son, currently seeking an associate position

1. Make clear whether small children are welcome for the in-person visit. Make childcare available if both parents are to be involved (e.g., house hunting, tour of community, etc.)

2. If small children are welcome, offer them a small token of recognition and appreciation (e.g., a storybook, stuffed animal, snacks— nothing expensive, but just be thoughtful). This welcoming spirit goes a long way with the parents!

3. Is the committee self-aware enough to know whether they desire true honesty from candidates or prefer formulated answers (just playing the game). Recheck your honesty levels and find a way to communicate that.

4. Does the committee understand the strengths and, also, areas of needed growth when hiring a young clergy person/family? (e.g., high energy levels, tons of creative ideas, likely lacking experience in conflict resolution.

5. Is the congregation aware of any gender bias they may have?

6. Staying with a church family on a visit is awkward! And, it doesn't allow any or at least much time to contemplate or have conversation between candidates and their partners.

7. A fancy hotel room is not necessary, especially if there isn't going to be any reimbursement for travel. Initiate the offer to do so when you make invitation.

8. Allow the candidates opportunity to help shape the itinerary during visits. What do they want to know or need to know about the wider community? Often, scheduling time with a realtor, just to drive around/talk about the community, provides outside perspective; and is, most often, better than a congregant tour.

9. Be wary if any one of the committee members dominates conversation without hesitation...red flag! Pay attention to your internal dynamics; the candidate is!

10. Take a moment to communicate with the candidates... Let them know where you are in the process and when you plan to contact them again. Don't leave them hanging!

From a previous senior minister/married woman currently serving as a co-minister in a new position

1. Please communicate with all your candidates! Know that this is a very stressful and sometimes lonely process for candidates. It is filled with a lot of waiting. Being clear about your timeline and when you will be following up is so helpful and relieves a lot of anxiety. Also, make sure you communicate if any timeline changes occur. And, when you are no longer interested in a candidate, please let them know ASAP. It is hard to do and no fun to hear, but it is even worse to have an interview and then hear nothing. You might think: "That doesn't happen," but it has! Multiple times! Courtesy is much appreciated.

2. The search and call process is like online dating. It can be awkward at times, but the goal is to get to know each other and see how you might fit together.

3. When you narrow to one candidate, show how you care about that candidate and his or her interests. The best thing a search committee recently did for me was take an interest in my areas of interest and ask about special skills/ training that I've pursued. They wanted to learn all they could about me, and that was mutual.

Encouragement

Most of God's good work gets done by folks who have already done a good day's work by the time they get to church. Serving on the search team is well above and way beyond the call of duty. Your efforts will write a new chapter in your church's life and mission. Your decisions will create a new ministerial partnership to guide and bless your church for years.

No pressure, right? You should be feeling it right about now. This may well be the single most important decision the congregation makes for some time to come. The reason it feels heavy is that there *is* a sobering weightiness to this task. It requires attentiveness to due process and a renewed communal commitment to prayer. Now is a great time to form a prayer team devoted to supporting this effort.

A certain humility is required for search team work, a certain willingness to suspend judgment and hold a certain groundedness—to be "of the earth" and rooted in place and in faithful trust. Here are some other spiritual qualities to be lauded:

1. Willingness to "not know" and be open to learn.

2. Good faith cooperation with the process requirements in a prayerful mindset.

3. Spiritual stability that keeps faith and steady resilience even when nothing seems to be working out.

4. Patience to listen not just until it's your turn to speak, but at the deeper levels of heart and soul; listening deeply, all the way down to the heart of the core issues.

5. Devotion that trusts the Holy Spirit to do that which only the Spirit can do.

6. Prayerful imagination that holds in the heart of God the paradox of congregational life. (By this I mean owning up before God to all that you are as a congregation—and all that you are not! Let's face it: humans are a tangled web of inconsistency and contradiction, yet beloved.)

7. Attending to the task and to each other with a spirit of joy, zest, and adventure.

One search team chair was driving home after an initial "ground rules" meeting that got rather intense, and this prayer came to mind:

"Lord, as I drive home tonight, somewhere there is a pastor who is heading home from a long day and an even longer evening meeting and thinking: 'Maybe what I can do here is done. It's been a good run, a fruitful season; maybe I should consider a fresh call.' Lord, might we be the answer to this prayer? Could we be the very challenge needed next? May your mysterious mercy make it so. Amen."

Confidentiality Covenant

Effective search teams begin building trust and community from the very moment they are asked to serve. Trust is the bond of mutual fidelity we create by what we choose to do with what is said within our confidential conversations. Trust doesn't just happen. It must be cultivated and only arises out of confidentiality. The World War II motto still applies: "Loose lips sink ships." Leaky search teams lose the congregation's trust—especially so when everyone in the pew seems to already have insider information on the top candidates and current search status before the team even reports. Agreement around what confidentiality means often reveals awkward places where our church family enmeshment needs a bit of untangling.

Search teams require candid, explicit conversation with full verbal agreement around the definitions of clarity and accountability. Nothing leaves the room. Ever. It all lives here and remains when we walk out. No heavy hints at home. No carrying papers out that might innocently be left somewhere. (Keep all papers, including your notes, in a locked cabinet in the church.) Please agree that at the first sign of discord, there will be no dragging out confidential information as ammunition for a kitchen sink church fight. "Never disclosed" means *never*.

Silly as it may seem for grown adults to go slowly around the room and explicitly invite each and every team member to offer an audible, verbal assent to the consensus definition of "confidential," this is what is necessary to create a confidentiality covenant. Think of it this way. When you elect to sit in the emergency exit row on an airplane, the flight attendant requires an out-loud, verbal consent that you understand and agree to the requirements and responsibilities of sitting in that row. A head nod will not suffice. Airlines do not *yet* need written and notarized statements or require blood oath covenants...but...well... Get the drift?

How will you create a safe holding space for sacred conversation? Spell out the details of your confidentiality covenant, then go around the room asking each other: "Is there any part of 'nothing leaves the room' that is unclear to you?" Spell it all out in your context. I know it is sounds sophomoric, but I urge you to engage in the full conversation. This means no pillow talk or even pillow *hints*. Not to your spouse, soul mate, or best friend. No jesting or jousting that reveals anything more than what the search team has publicly said. And, after the search team is successful and a call is extended, no tattling out of school or after school. *One last point:* There is no time limit or expiration date on this trust clause. It strains Christian unity and charity when search team deliberations show up in a heated board meeting six months after the call. While you are binding each other in sacred trust, make sure you agree on how long this confidentiality bond holds.

I know it is tedious to be this explicit, but the next step is to hold each other accountable. Blow the whistle and call strict fouls on this matter or your search team may foul out before it can even put any points on the board. Consider forging this relational agreement as team homework. Some search teams actually hammer out a signed covenant of confidentiality. I know of search teams who did not come to firm agreement around their own definition of confidentiality and were a leaky sieve as a result. After several warnings, the board chair finally had to dismiss and reconstitute the entire team. It was an embarrassment that humbled and haunted them, yet it revealed gossip dynamics that explained a history of gaffes that had long plagued the congregation's communication. What does your team need to create a group atmosphere in which this mutual understanding is not only official policy but an honored and covenanted agreement? Furthermore, does the congregation understand and agree to not pester or pry information? Sometimes in reaction to the accusation that the team is too secretive or too slow it may be tempting to appease expectations for prompt results by leaking little tidbits and hints. This is a huge no-no. Simply smile and quote the standard wisdom: "These days a 'normal' search process often takes 12–18 months."

Before your team even gets off the ground, some folks will already be asking, "Are you done yet? If not, why not?" Take a proactive approach and communicate process, progress, and numbers, but no names, places, or any identifiable hints. One team posted their progress in writing and worship announcements until they were nearly sick of hearing themselves communicate. Only then had they barely begun to have the congregation's attention. Remember the congregation is about five repetitions of communication behind your present progress, so allow extra lead time for those who are "slow to hear but ever swift to speak" to catch up.

One search team made valiant efforts to over-communicate, only to discover the anxiety level of the congregation was such that whatever information the team offered was not enough, and only prompted more angst. Imagine anxious inquiry as opportunity to reinforce core values, common dreams, and the kinds of things you hope the congregation knows about itself. When people ask, this is also a good time to elicit intercessory prayers.

If all this sounds stark raving rabid and way over the edge, you are getting the point. Spare your team future agony and spell confidentiality out on the front end. If you have a leak, address it now or it may bite you at a most inopportune moment. I press this point out of sad experiences where excellent candidates, who may well have been a great congregational match, got spooked and withdrew from candidacy when leaks traced to the search team set the denominational grapevine jangling. *Reminder:* You are not just shuffling hunks of paper here. These conversations affect some minister's career, family, and future. Please ponder and puzzle out your confidentiality covenant as a group exercise, and then handle with loving care.

The Start Line

All right, the members of your search team have been invited to serve and have accepted. You have been duly appointed and officially installed. You have completed the detailed documents profiling your congregation for candidates. Your judicatory leaders have met with the team to orient, inform, and educate them regarding all necessary due process. You are now ready for the next phase.

In addition to your official congregational profile, consider creating for candidates a zippy, fun presentational version of who you are as a congregation. Introduce yourself as you would like to be introduced; featuring all your best selling points. In a sudden burst of energetic imagination, send your potential candidates a five-minute video or an illustrated script built around context, history, and significant ministry achievements. You don't have to oversell, but most churches fail to boldly, joyfully witness to the awesome grace of being who they are before God. Don't hold back in demonstrating your passion for God's work. Reveal more of the "real you" than a candidate might glean from your website.

WARNING: You do not want to get caught offering this awkward excuse to your first serious candidate: "Well, our website needs a little updating." If it's not ready, neither are you!

Preoccupation with your process takes over and it's easy to forget there is a delicate parallel process at work. Candidates are sorting piles of congregational profiles while your search team sifts through candidate resumes. How will yours stand out? As you shape those first impressions you hope to project, consider throwing into the mix a fun video clip portraying your "ideal" minister. Move over Wonder Woman or Clark Kent! Spice it up a little bit. Have fun. *Note:* Fun *is* allowed. In case you missed the memo, a light touch of levity was issued with your "hunting license." Permission granted. Humorous encounters help us counter all the unconscious expectations that need to be peeled off the pastor's back and the congregation's back as well. Since there are no perfect congregations or pastors, humor helps break the power of unrealistic projection. We humans are such suckers for neurotic perfection. It is so often our undoing, is it not? It helps open healthy conversation when we bring fantastic expectations into a realm where we can own up, laugh at ourselves, and be restored to the sanity and sobriety of what is possible under the conditions of our existence.

Make It Fun

Hopefully, the process of team building runs parallel with the time it takes to create the congregational profile and gather candidate names. I hope you are sensing the surrounding grace of prayers and congregational confidence. You are the best team your church can field. That said, is there any way to allow yourselves to also enjoy being church? Can you take the task seriously, but yourselves not so much? How might the grace of a light touch actually energize your team's work? While you ponder over all these volumes of forgotten lore (i.e., resumes), keep an eye out for any enjoyable ironies. How might you appreciate the humor surrounding such a solemn task? Pay attention and make it fun. Just because it is church doesn't mean it has to be drudgery. Life is too short and precious to not have some fun with these rare moments.

One search team who effectively created spiritual community and bonded well admitted their own surprise at how much they enjoyed the process of getting to know each other. Their sense of community carried over to the candidates and led to an effective call. The team bonded around sharing their spiritual autobiographies. This kind of deeper listening, appreciating, and honoring sets the tone for how to receive a candidate's story. There is no way the zest of your search team's lives can fail to communicate vitality and good vibrations to candidates. Ministers have built-in radar that raises alarm when a search team is "out of sync." If the team hasn't gelled, unconscious signals are emitted—something like: "We are not really as familiar with our church or each other or the process as we need to be in order to function smoothly." It sends a clear message, but not a good one.

Here are some additional qualities a ministerial candidate might hope for in a search team:

1. Authenticity and transparency

2. b) Evidence of mission passion and spiritual integrity

3. c) Well-grounded in faith and practice

4. d) Witness to devotion and deeper commitment

5. d) Good relationships between team members

6. e) Signs that they can have fun

Your team's spiritual synergy radiates discernible energy. Positive dynamics attract the kind of leader you will follow, enjoy serving beside, want to partner with, and genuinely respect.

Will you figure out what motivates and energizes your team and invest deeply in the process, and each other? Energy invested now increases later yield. So, invest in each other, make the search as much fun as you can stand to have in church,…and…invest in prayer.

The Work of Prayer

Every church has a few folks who are informally known as the "go to" people for prayer. If you were standing in the need of prayer, who in the church would you call on? Call on them! They need not be privy to the gritty details of the search process in order to offer intercession. The work of calling a minister cannot be solely predicated on a business model. Get some prayer energies going. Perhaps the elders or spiritual leaders might declare a day of prayer. Maybe the church could designate a day or time of the day/week to devote to prayer support? There's also a lot to be said for the clarity that fasting brings. If fasting seems too far out for your taste, you may want to survey Scripture on this topic. Sometimes a brief season of fasting from media and technology allows deeper levels of clarity and singular focus on essential mission to emerge.

You don't really know someone until you have prayed with that person. Even if you have cooked and served in the church kitchen or gone on mission trips together, prayer is what binds the tie that binds. Praying with your team, both silently and aloud around the circle, is a modest start. Carve out the time needed in order for prayer to move beyond polite and perfunctory levels. Listen in the silence between the words. Attend the conversation as it ripens and deepens. At the end of each candidate interview, before beginning the inevitable plunge into analysis, keep silence for a bit. It's not just the words that count. The space between the words is where spirits—human and holy—commune.

What you are attempting in prayer is something Jesus admitted rarely happens among us: agreement. Perhaps that's the reason Jesus promised the moon to his disciples in answered prayer (Mt. 18:18–19). Jesus knew how complicated it would be—well nigh impossible—for humans to deeply agree on much of anything, let alone the calling of a pastor. . The formation and confirmation of a call are profound examples of a rare communion of hearts arising out of this deep "yes" in the Spirit.

Gathering Names

Every name and resume of a candidate coming via official channels deserves thoughtful attention. First, it's good practice in reading between the lines. Second, these candidates are supposed to be prescreened and vetted, in good standing with your ecclesiastical body, and cleared on criminal background checks. These systemic precautions are built-in protections. It is to your advantage to fully understand both how your call system operates *optimally* and how it, *in fact,* often works. Ask questions and pose "for instances" until you begin to get a feel for how the system operates in theory and practice. Learn what the system can tell you and what it can't. This is the zone of operation for your call process, and your middle judicatory leaders are the brokers of this system. The more you learn, the better served you will be.

Once the formal search is announced, don't be surprised when candidates appear out of the wild blue. Expect names to magically appear, well outside the formal process. Aunt Mabel's nephew-in-law just finished training at a school nobody's every heard of and she submits his name. *My advice:* exercise caution. There may be undisclosed and legally undisclosable reasons why a minister is not candidating through the system. There may be good cause around why no one has ever heard of someone. Explore the surrounding circumstances and probe to find out why a candidate may not be in good standing. You need to know if a minister is under some disciplinary action or probationary period. There's an art to reading dossiers; get educated. While the team may weary of reading reams of profile papers, the upside is that it sharpens your perceptive capacity. By the way, I would think long and hard about going beyond the system to accept candidates and endorsements when there is no feasible way to verify character, investigate issues or allegations, get a glimpse into spiritual formation, or glean history on ordination and work habits, ethic, and history. Also bear in mind that there are always excellent candidates who are in good standing, but not currently active in the search process and happily serving elsewhere. They will not appear in the stacks of active candidate dossiers. While you may be officially discouraged from pursuing such persons, they are fair game. If you have reason to believe there is a good match between what they are gifted to do and what you need done, it never hurts to make discrete inquiry.

Search teams sometimes complain that the pool of qualified candidates who might match their needs and context is extremely limited. People dream about methods to end run the system in order to secure more names of potential candidates. The better play is to learn the game within the system—better known as networking. My advice is to network, then work it, work it, work it! Sadly, during the search process, a congregation may discover just how disconnected and isolated they have become from life and ministry in the wider church. They may have no clue about recent trends, fresh perspectives, or who shows promise as an upcoming leader. There is wisdom in keeping your congregation's wider church networks in good repair. You don't know you need them until you need them.

Yikes! Skype

If you don't know what Skype is, you may not be quite ready to interview live candidates yet. Get immersed in the pool of technology. This is still awkward stuff for far too many churches. I know it seems like only yesterday that we finally mastered that clumsy old telephone conference call box as we hunkered around the church library table to conduct candidate phone interviews. Now there's some new technology that appears light years beyond our present capability? By whatever technology you choose to communicate, master the technology first. This may sound like a no-brainer, but candidates frequently report frustration around the gawky way cyber interviews are conducted. Poor connections, bad lighting, awkward staging, and intermittent technical interference do not add up to an A-list impression. While search teams often seem to seek candidates in their early 30s with 40 years experience, consider the flip side: most younger clergy are tech savvy, so how you handle interview communication is one of their Rorschach tests. Never doubt that you, too, are being checked out.

Once the team has been oriented, prepped, and prepared for the interview process, we are ready to consider candidates. The first order of business is to determine a potential candidate's level of interest. (BTW: the initial contact is often done on your behalf by the middle judicatory) Once you have established a contact list in which there is mutual interest and a priority order, you begin to reach out and make calls to get acquainted, determine genuine interest level, and schedule a phone or Skype interview. In preparation for this, create a seating chart depicting each member of the team (maybe a recent picture with a few lines of bio) and send this to the candidate in advance of the call. Remember to sit in those predesignated spots during all interviews. Such a simple courtesy smoothes the whole process for interviewer and interviewee. Logistical ease helps the interview move more readily into areas of detail and depth.

Strategize ways to address the imbalance of information. While you have the candidates' full detailed dossiers, all they are working with are your church profile and a brief conversation with the middle judicatory or maybe a preliminary phone call with the search team chair to determine level of interest. The spirit and manner in which you provide information is a way of demonstrating your ability, capacity, and personality to a prospective pastor. You are naturally so focused on getting the right candidate that it is easy to forget about being the right congregation for the candidate. In church governance systems where congregational call formats are operative, both parties are interviewing.

In the interview process, consider coordinating your questions to avoid a scattergun approach. Asking the same questions to all interviewees makes correlating all their responses easier. In the interest of efficiency, some interview teams and candidates exchange initial questions beforehand. There is no significant advantage to playing a game of "stump the chump." Trick questions can backfire; save them for in-person interviews when you can watch their eyebrows (i.e., full body language and nonverbals). You may also want to think through how to shape a strong ending to the interview. Some interview teams just can't seem to find a stopping point, and the energy just dribbles away. Not good. Nail a strong positive ending. Even a simple prayer for mutual discernment followed by a sincere expression of appreciation ends the conversation on an up note. Maybe something like this:

"Lord, thank you for being in our midst for blessing; for coming by and being our rabbi during this hour. Now we pray: shepherd this conversation. Lead us by the still waters where your voice may be heard. If this is indeed a call, let the intrigue linger. If not, make it plain. Either way we bless you for this pastor, knowing we are all but servants of The Servant, in whose name we pray. Amen."

What makes a good interview perfect is practice. This may feel slightly contrived, but I recommend practice interviews. Invite a minister who is clearly not a candidate and can keep a secret to practice honing your skills. Do a lively mock interview. Shoot your questions, practice reading responses. Afterward, debrief the whole process with the faux candidate. You may be surprised how this kind of live-feedback loop helps take the fumbles out of that first round of interviews. *Note:* This is fair game for ministers too. I have gamed these practice interviews often enough to know it loosens up the conversation. Also, get some strong, insightful questions to lead in breaking the ice. (*Note:* See "20 Questions" on page 86 for some examples)

Speaking of practice, your team needs to practice sharing, in a comfortable and knowledgeable way, some specific, concrete examples of how your mission, vision, and key values show up in church life. When, how, and where does your congregation's core DNA come up off the page and get lived out? Can you illustrate this dynamic with brief, poignant examples? Using a broad brush, lift the major themes. Let your candidate feel the pulse, the congregation's heartbeat. Learn to do this effectively in an hour-long interview. You would be surprised how rusty and out of practice many search teams come across to candidates. Dull, tired interviews do not draw energy; they drain it. Master the interview process from your end. If you want maximum effect, put your best foot forward. Sloppy, unfocused interviews produce candidates somewhat interested but not overly impressed. You can do something to shape these critical first impressions. While you are occupied with qualifying candidates for the finals, you may not get past their first round options. So practice!

Site Visit Itinerary

Once you have cleared the hurdles of first round interviews and emerged with a prioritized list of candidates, you are ready to extend on-site invitations. In preparation for the live, on-site visit by a candidate, consider creating a provisional itinerary with selected activities that optimize the candidate's time, showcase the advantages of the wider community and present the positive energies of your ministry setting. Send a written itinerary in advance for his or her confirmation, along with the assurance you will make all arrangements and cover all expenses; all the candidate need do is show up. Extend your hospitality beyond the church building. At the hotel, create a little welcome basket stocked with local amenities. This doesn't need to be major swag, just a warm and thoughtful way to keep saying, "We value your visit and thanks for taking the time." Quaint as this rather old-fashioned concept may seem to postmodern sensibilities, you *are* courting.

It can get logistically tricky to arrange a tightly packed whirlwind visit while maintaining low profile anonymity. If possible, consider hosting the initial get-acquainted interview and meal in a member's home rather than a restaurant. Candidates frequently complain that way too much of the interview evening is lost in a commercial atmosphere not conducive to the level of intimate, cozy conversation required for discernment. Some teams bypass these issues by arranging the first visit on some neutral ground that allows greater privacy and opens up more psychic space for purposeful and prayerful conversations. *The point?* Get a handle on the atmosphere, and make it work to your advantage. This simple, basic advice often goes unheeded. Don't get bogged down in concerns that are secondary to the connection and conversation.

Along this same lines, I am astonished to learn how many search teams move through a rather rigorous interview process without ever creating a space for an unhurried session of quiet prayer led by the candidate. This might take the form of an almost Quaker-style quiet worship, as you simply sit together in the Presence to gain some sense of the meeting of minds and hearts in the heart of God. If the search process truly is a mutual discernment of call and not just another hire, how else would we get to know each other's souls? If discernment of call truly is a matter that plumbs the depth of the heart, how do we create a moment when we touch into this place where we all "live and move and have our being"? Let's move beyond creating favorable first impressions. Of course, we have to have the latter to gain the former. Beyond some supernatural sign in letters of fire fourteen feet high, the only way I know to be assured of the spiritual basis of a mutual call is to actually share time in prayerful conversation. Seek some mutual sense of spiritual agreement aimed at creating the basis for a solid sense of ministry partnership.

What Does Spiritual Agreement Look Like?

Agree with whom? About what? Do I have to like you in order to agree? What if we have had some tiffs over the years, found ourselves on opposite sides of church life and now, ironically, end up on the search team together? Yikes! No irony deficiency here! Is it time for a cup of coffee and a side conversation? We don't have to be buddy-buddy. If we cannot release past offenses and present irritations and come to some mutual meeting of the minds for the sake of the call process, misery abounds. Think "hung jury."

In terms of team internal dynamics, the core agreement is critical. If the makeup of your team can demonstrate diversity without divisiveness, it will be a huge blessing. Each individual member is responsible for his or her measure of equanimity, if not plain peaceableness, within the whole team. Remember, you don't have to see eye to eye to walk shoulder to shoulder. Seriously, how *are* you with each other? Establishing our deepest agreement may well require some "come to Jesus" moments. This is an apt description—it's awfully hard to discern the mind of Christ when you want to give other team members a piece of yours. Examine resentments, release hurts and slights, engage enthusiasms, and express gratitudes. Learn to enjoy the journey and the company.

Spiritual agreement is an offering of three wholehearted "yeses." The first yes is to God in surrender and hope. The second yes is to each other, recognizing we are bound beyond our differences to a higher purpose. The third yes aims at mutual discernment around the decision at hand. When we treat the search team process strictly as a personnel task, using a business model, then the focus flattens to "just get 'er done!" While efficiency and effectiveness have their place, they are not paramount. We need to attend to the delicate balance between task orientation and the process of melding minds and hearts in higher mutual purpose. Admittedly, the process of getting to agreement is tedious and some days require more than we are willing to give! But even that confession is a sign of progress! Authentic agreement seems to require mutual confession as we learn to appreciate the efforts made to get to "yes" with each other.

Three elements converge to create spiritual agreement: mutual availability, mutual vulnerability, and mutual accountability. A good start might be searching our collective heart before God as we listen deeply to each other, the Spirit, the Word, and quiet prayer. A measure of personal vulnerability is necessary for a positive process and a fruitful result. We also need to meet each other in personal disclosure appropriate to the issues. This is the kind of spiritual exercise that keeps us all heart-healthy.

Let's look at the dynamic of agreement from the candidate's side. Woe betide the minister who, seven months into accepting a new call, learns that the search team glossed over several major fissures and fractures in congregational life. All the hard work of adjustment agonies, the uprooting and resettling the family, and the real estate issues feel like a slap in the face. We are talking here about matters never named or acknowledged, let alone addressed in the interview process or early orientation and adjustment period. There was never any agreement on how these matters might be handled going forward. Now these issues surface in an unhealthy way, as obstacles to getting ministry traction and advancing the mission.

Suppose during the interview process, there were signs indicating the congregation's tectonic plates had slipped a fraction. I'm talking about those slight rumbling sounds that signal underground conflict. Instead of pausing to explore, the search team elected to ignore these tremors. Six months into the new pastorate, still in formative stages, momentum is already beginning to stall. The truth inevitably surfaces. The new pastor now experiences the search team's earlier avoidance as more than just a little "judicious ducking." It begins to look like a case of outright denial of conflict issues. The cognitive dissonance raises doubt about just how deliberate this oversight may have been. Are we looking at betrayal of trust? It opens the question: "And what else haven't you told me?"

The breach widens as spiritual agreement fractures and attitudes unravel a bit. Before deterioration sets in, take the time to rediscover why spiritual agreement is so hard won and dicey to maintain. Getting back into agreement means mutually acknowledging the breach, owning up and working through. "Through" is the only way to go now, but think what a different conversation this might have been if there had been fuller disclosure on the front end. There is a difference between airing dirty laundry and recognizing that wash day is a weekly occurrence. You want to be transparent about the issues, opportunities, and challenges that are unique to your congregation. Straight talk is needed here. (OK, let's try the shoe on the other foot. Sometimes congregations learn, after the fact, things about their new minister that make them more than a bit uncomfortable. Now what? See what I mean about the necessity of mutual disclosure and spiritual agreement?)

According to Thom Ranier of Lifeway Research "Facts and Trends" Report, the average tenure of Protestant ministers is 3.6 years. Trevin Wax (General Baptist blog) estimates the average tenure at 5 to 7 years. Among Disciples of Christ pastors, nearly 60% have tenures under 5 years (salary research at indianadisciples.org). In contrast to these pastoral tenure statistics, I know of no studies on the longevity of tenure for search team members. In my experience, if half of the search team members are still active five years into the pastor's tenure, it's indication of a good match. Because search teams disband once the call is accepted, with a few members transitioning to a pastoral relations team, these retention rates would be much harder to track than pastors. The question remains: What might retention rates among search team members tell us about the effectiveness of the search process?

How Are You Praying?

The discipline and devotion that assists discernment is rarely named as a critical factor in the search process. You might introduce this conversation by inviting the search team to describe some of the practices that assist their sense of presence with and for God. What are the spiritual practices you each engage? Quiet scripture reading? Meditation? Prayer-walking? *Lectio divina*? Tai chi? Chai Tea? Knitting? Spiritual direction? Yoga? Accountability partners? Silence?

I'm not suggesting that saying our prayers is some sort of lucky rabbit's foot. This whole process is full of a grace that we cannot earn or evoke by incantation. Our prayer practices attune our souls to a sense of Presence, yet seldom do we share candid conversation around the care and feeding of our own souls. We are extraordinarily reticent to reveal our deepest devotion, but here's why this matters. Let's say you attend the search team meetings, taking up space, breathing the shared air, but spiritually you are skimming the surface and not really engaged in any rhythm of prayer or devotion that heightens your spiritual awareness. If you are coasting, not growing in your spiritual life, then when the chips are down and it's decision time, you have no cogent Word, no relevant inspiration, no illuminating guidance to offer. All you have is your opinion, and the broth of opinion usually makes a mighty thin soup. Or, using the imagery of Psalm 1:4, our ego-driven opinions are "like chaff that the wind drives away." Prayer practices help us sift the wheat of discernment from chaff of opinion. A search team that creates spiritual community based on shared devotion gains the gift of discernment, and the core maturity to sift opinions from deeper illuminations. This is why it is important that we find gracious, gentle ways to invite team conversation and mutual disclosure around what assists our sense of God's presence in our work.

Getting to Yes

Somewhere amidst the process, a search team takes on a life of its own. This is not just another church group meeting. The team's gathering, listening, and praying becomes "church." The collective willingness to carry conversation into unexplored depths, to ponder possibilities to linger and creatively brood, opens up deeper wellsprings inside us and among us. Spirits—human and holy—converge and commune. Quakers speak of the "dawning of the light"; Pentecostals, about a "holy spirit moment." Whatever terms you use, convergence and confirmation around a call is the fruit of taking time to care for one another, pacing the process and evaluating progress through reflective conversation and ever-deepening listening. I call this "honoring the Spirit" by listening deeply for the Christ in you to meet the Christ in me. The Presence among us manifests in peaceable, unifying ways. Where the Spirit of the Lord is, there is an unusual liberty, a freedom that enlarges the capacity to speak directly to the hearts of one another regarding illuminations we perceive through quiet communal prayer. This is not business as usual. The call arises as deep calls unto deep. This is the spiritual convergence that witnesses, clarifies, and confirms a sense of call.

Within the context of this trustfulness, doubts may arise. These are what I call a "check in the spirit." Maybe a bit of conversation still lingers at the corner of your mind... *What did the candidate mean by that?* Sometimes an unvoiced question begs asking. Maybe a tiny doubt wiggles and nibbles at the edge of consciousness. Maybe this "check" arises around a remark that did not sit right with you, and you wonder if that was "your stuff" getting in the way (again), or hints of unsurfaced issues. Maybe it was a passing comment that did not quite pass muster, that should have triggered further follow-up but was not pursued. Sometimes a slight reservation you thought was resolved simply will not accede to easy dismissal. Sometimes you want a particular candidate to "be the one" so badly that you answer all possible objections or reservations on that person's behalf in your own mind. These may be matters that never come to the surface in the team conversation; it all happens in your head. These are the kinds of things that could comprise a "check in the spirit," a caution flag. In the words of that ancient arbiter of rules, *Robert's Rules of Order,* this is unfinished business.

First, you should check yourself out, asking, "Is this just me? Do I have issues?" (Most of us not only have issues, but a whole subscription, right?) *So, is this internal sticking point mainly my own unresolved stuff surfacing? Should I take a chance to voice my nagging concern when the team momentum already seems to be swinging in favor of calling a candidate?* It's quite humbling to admit we each still have issues that trigger us. This is better known as "being human." Giving voice to such a "check in your spirit" allows everyone the opportunity to check their own assumptions, to review and restate their common understanding: "Are we in agreement? How deep is the foundation of our agreement? Are we missing something? Is there any need for further investigation? How might we address these heretofore nameless natterings? Can we identify our fears and clarify risks?"

While this may seem like a sidebar to the task of calling, these little excursions often provide occasion for sharper articulation of your mission, helping you unpack your assumptions, clarify your common vision and push you to own the core values that drive you as a congregation. Granted, sometimes sidebars are just rabbit trails. Have a good laugh and hop back on track. Just don't dismiss objections and concerns too easily.

The search process lurches forward by fits and starts, fueled by questions and curiosities. Sometimes it takes a thorough exploration of a "check in the spirit" to finally confirm that you are on the right track or that you need to slow down and scope things out. Trustful transparency and soul-searching may not feel like prayer, but this difficult conversation is actually a means of moving you all toward fuller agreement, leading to a kind of communal confirmation out of which consensus may arise. Trust your collective instincts to lead in the discovery of other things you may need to know to make a good call. Consider the possibility that even this conversation is prayer. For those of us who think of prayer in the traditional modality of hands folded and eyes closed, addressing God alone, this might be an opportunity to expand our practice of prayer. Many search teams share this kind of prayerful conversation in working toward full agreement.

Negotiating Terms of Call

No matter how often I listen as pastors discern a call or leaders issue a call, I never cease to be amazed at the particulars and peculiarities. How do circumstances converge to confirm a call? To me, the whole process is a bit of a brilliant mystery. I am in awe of the stunning idea that God would use people (whose finitude, faults, flaws, foibles, and frailties are ever before them), to call a minister, equally flawed, for a higher, holy purpose beyond both of them, which is best fulfilled in a ministry partnership. A snippet of scripture hints at this process. Acts 15:28 says: "For it has seemed good to the Holy Spirit and to us to…" Again, there is the hint of communion with spirits human and holy. Again, the convergence of context and conversation impinges on the discernment that drives choices.

The mighty mystery comes home to roost when it is time to capture on a piece of paper this deeply wrought agreement. Here's where we begin to "scrute" the inscrutable. There remains this matter of making the call official in your denominational system and documenting the detail in a letter defining the Terms of Call. This prompts frank and often lively conversation around what constitutes compensation, additional benefits, and special arrangements. The question is:

How do we put a monetary value on the potential we see in this call? Once the "meeting of the hearts" takes place, we trust that a "meeting of the minds" will follow.

Two matters must be addressed: (a) What is the congregation capable of providing? And (b) What will be necessary to make the minister's life work?

While not an absolute, it is often helpful if at least one member of the search team is a professional in financial matters such as salary, benefits, and tax packages, and can bridge conversations with the church's administrative board and finance committee regarding such matters. *The main thing:* Don't let someone's misunderstanding of the arrangements skew the deal. Work it through until everyone does more than just nods; make sure they understand, agree, and verbally support it. You might be surprised how often trying to save a few thousand dollars will gum up the works and create bad feelings. Let generosity of spirit and mutual good will predominate in these critical conversations.

Part of the preliminary conversation around compensation is to clarify what is included in the often-used term "the total package." While this is a traditional way churches frame the conversation, it is also misleading and outmoded. I advise we eliminate the term "total package." *Here's why:* The "total package" concept has been totaled. It's a wrecked concept. By it, the congregation usually means: total impact on the budget's bottom line. Candidates see it more as: what I need to make my life work. You are not on the same page yet. These are different numbers.

Newly ordained pastors consistently report: "My seminary experience did not prepare me for hammering out the details of my compensation package." To be fair, they likely heard a lecture on the basic building blocks and principles, but maybe missed the subtleties of how to strategically move the pieces around the board in the actual process of negotiation. This is often a painfully difficult conversation for the vast majority of young pastors (and some older ones too!). Most pastors have trouble defining their material needs in explicit numerical terms, and most congregations have folks quite skilled at talking about money. This doesn't sound like a level playing field, does it?

Creating common ground begins with building a consensual framework as baseline for this admittedly awkward conversation. *Again, the bad news:* The "total package" idea doesn't accurately reflect the true total costs of doing ministry. *The good news:* If you can mutually agree on some shared principles of compensation *before* detailing negotiations, both minister and search team can build a foundation of trust that will carry you through the stickier points.

Point of AGREEMENT #1: Defining the total cost of doing business.

The total cost to doing ministry is fairly divided into two sub-categories:

A. The personal monies a minister receives for his or her work, primarily salary and housing. A minister may elect to direct a portion of salary as deferred compensation in the form of a tax-deferred annuity, Roth, or benefit accumulation/savings account. These instruments are often available through the denomination's pension fund. Saving money is a solid spiritual practice to start early, and puts a young pastor on the upside of compound interest. This is critical because today's pastors, like all young professionals, enter into a career with accumulated debt from student loans. Credit card debt also erodes any positive net gain from income.

B. The full expense a church incurs in calling a minister. Benefits are included in the church's cost of doing business because they occur no matter who the minister is. In addition to salary and housing, which are the personal compensation (part A above) there are other considerations that include health care, accident insurance, a health savings account, pension, social security, state income tax, continuing education and convention attendance, cell phone, all church-related hospitality, computer/Internet, vacation, sabbatical, study leave, moving expenses, and providing a vehicle or covering all travel expenses. These are the congregation's cost of doing the business of ministry, not strictly compensation.

I always cringe when I see a laundry list of items that are actually the church's cost of doing business being crammed into the minister's "package." So before you quote any numbers, come to a mutual agreement that fairly delineates "cost of doing church business" from personal compensation. Let's compare apples with apples. The sum of these two categories presents the fullest accounting of the cost of ministry for the minister and the congregation to serve their mission together.

Point of AGREEMENT #2: Being fair all around.

While the sum of those "costs of doing business" (part B above) is certainly a consideration for the congregation in arriving at the final amount it will elect to offer the minister (part A above); it is not fair for the congregation to expect the minister to personally bear the costs (and tax consequences) that occur from doing the church's business. Nor is it fair for the minister to inflate the personal salary section of the equation knowing they will have to cover anticipated expenses of doing ministry. The best negotiations begin with the congregation and minister defining mutual fiscal responsibility.

Point of AGREEMENT #3: Mutual clarity.

Agreed: It will not cost the minister money out of pocket to do the church's business. Standard business practice does not require this kind of "in-kind contribution" from employees. Churches need to follow standard practice, and develop reporting protocols that minimize tax consequences for the minister. Many churches provide a church credit card for the pastor's use for church expenses. The details of this will likely involve consultation with a tax accountant who understands current IRS law. Denominational offices also offer general guidance.

Point of AGREEMENT # 4: Researching and updating.

Compensation research often provides a more balanced perspective. Rather than simply offering the new pastor a standard percentage less than the previous pastor as a starting point, find out if the church's offer is competitive in the local market. Consider community research on local salary scales, income information provided by the state government, and personal conversations about vocations comparably compensated. How do salary scales jibe with costs of living? Would other local churches be willing to confidentially disclose the statistical basis on which they scale compensation? One previously helpful reference point was a study of salary comparisons with school principals. Typically, they have similar educational requirements and hold similar public trust. Unfortunately, in most communities, this old comparison is no longer applicable; principals are paid considerably more! Maybe teachers at the top of their scale are a more realistic fit, especially if the salary scale includes doctorates.

When adjusting compensation ranges, take into account factors such as previous ministry experience, special gifts and talents, years of service, additional education, additional training, specialty business skills applicable to church life, and future educational plans. This is also a good time for the congregation to audit and review its own financial position, including debt service, analysis of giving levels and trends, attendance patterns, confidential assessment of giving potential, future ministry or major maintenance plans that involve capital expenditures, and projected local economic factors that may impact church income and operating expenses.

When was the last time you conducted a serious salary study? Generally speaking, generosity begets generosity and creates a positive money mindset for the church's financial leadership.

Again, before specific numbers are discussed, please have the preliminary conversation on these four points of agreement and come to some basic understanding in the search team and finance committee. Your conversation may modify and refine mutual understanding. If you strive to arrive at agreement around these principles before talking actual numbers, everybody starts the money conversation on the same page.

Another economic reality not always acknowledged is the fact that an average worship attendance of 150 is generally considered the breakpoint for supporting a full-time, seminary trained, ordained minister. That means many smaller congregations are feeling the squeeze of being "on the bubble" and forever juggling maintenance needs with ministry needs. This is a twenty-first–century reality looking for creative, entrepreneurial solutions.

Next Steps

Negotiating the nitty-gritty details of the Terms of Call letter to the reasonable satisfaction of all concerned makes for mutual trust and hope. So much of the money mindset is mutually revealed and provides a foundation for solid ministry partnership.

Once the Letter of Agreement is signed, the next steps include presenting the search team's recommendation to the church board. In some denominational polity, the elders or trustees are advised. Exercise special care to arrange the congregational meeting with all the proper notices. Even if the timing is a bit inconvenient, don't take any shortcuts here. Research the legalities on proper notifications so the decision cannot be submarined on some constitutional or by-laws technicality. You want unquestionable compliance here. Make sure this meeting is done "decently and in order," reflecting the full integrity and intention of both the congregation and the candidate.

Oh, yes, and by the way...somewhere along about now, be prepared for some pushback. While the search team cheers the checkered flag and is ready to enjoy a victory lap, be aware that the formal announcement of a call to be considered may trigger another wave of resistance, grief, confusion, and questioning. A new call means you are also closing a chapter of your congregation's life, facing some finality and finitude, and owning your present reality. Your former ministry chapter is now "former" for sure, and that first sniff of change in the air can bring on a sudden allergic reaction. Be as patient as you can, without allowing resistant reactions to damage the integrity of a call you have diligently discerned. Keep the process on track. The word is: steady on!

OK, so not everyone will appreciate or agree with the search team's recommendation. These objections may even feel like a slap in the face to the team. Find a way to not take this questioning and impugning of your integrity personally—it could be a great grace. The fact is, the congregation has not really been following your progress all that closely, until now. In terms of the communication loop, lag-time factors kick in. Folks in the pews are at least three or four steps behind your leadership. Bring them up to speed. Your gracious patience during the process of presenting the candidate most often yields positive results. You are not only presenting the results of your search, you are reacquainting and educating the congregation on the actual process. So you could be fielding objections based on a misunderstanding of the process itself as well as qualms about the actual candidate. With the possible exception of a few leaders who have served on previous search teams, the congregation has no realistic clue about the hours of conversation and prayer invested in your recommendation. The saying, "Never let them see you sweat," doesn't apply now. Let them see your sweat, blood, and tears. You have poured your time and energy into this search process and stand in full support of this recommendation. If you believe in this candidate and this pivotal moment, then the church needs to experience the witness of your heart, sense your enthusiasm, and share your reasons for rejoicing. Without defensiveness and with great joy, be ready to share your willing witness to a future you see.

I am trying to say that by the time you reach this stage of the process, you have a lot invested in this call. If you can avoid taking the congregation's questions as personal criticism and not get defensive, it will help the process immeasurably. Your nonanxious clarity and competence will clear the decks and get the search team out of the way so the congregation can get to know the candidate more directly. So, take their questions at face value and work through their concerns with candor and good humor. Appreciate their interest and gain their confidence without overselling. Try to build good will and forge agreement by giving the benefit of the doubt whenever you possibly can. Your team has been working out on the cutting edge, light years ahead of the congregation, projecting further into the future than most folks live. You've selected a pastoral leader whom you believe can carry the congregation forward; give the folks in the pews time to catch up.

While you don't want to cover up lingering congregational concerns with something glib like,

"Well, let's all go home and pray about it," this might actually be a good time to invoke prayer—especially thoughtful, conversational prayer. Recognize there may come a time when your search team needs to simply and directly say to folks who, even after reasonable assurance, still strenuously object to the call recommendation: "Then just vote 'no'—it's really OK!" As time for the congregational vote draws near, you finally have to give people the energy of their opinions and pray you all make room for the Holy Spirit.

Another "by the way": After your candidate choice is clear and your recommendation has been enthusiastically received by the board, but before the congregational vote, if you have not already done so, please release and notify all the other candidates you engaged in previous conversation. You should have already given them the courtesy of a heads up conversation earlier. Once you are clear that a candidate is not a good match, make it a habit to give him or her the courtesy of personal notification in as timely a manner as possible. I realize there is a certain measure of jockeying on the part of both candidates and search teams to assure the widest options for as long as possible. But holding a candidate in reserve in case the first choice doesn't pan out is just not fair.

These courtesy calls need not involve a long explanation, just respectful appreciation to the candidates for their time and interest. Because this is never an easy conversation, many search teams put off making call-backs. This leaves a lingering negative impression that can be easily avoided by buckling down to make those difficult calls and write those awkward letters. Handling this with prompt dispatch, and especially paying any unreimbursed travel expenses candidates may have incurred, is a positive witness for your congregation. Besides, you never know. In addition to good business practice, you may need a ministerial friend in the future. It's an opportunity for mutual good will.

Care and Feeding of Ministers

After the "t's" are crossed, the protocols complete, the votes counted, and the announcements readied, consider one final thing. As a member of the search team, you have an early opportunity to build a strong trust relationship with your new pastor. Now is not the time to back off and disappear into the church woodwork. So, ask yourself: What kind of personal commitment have you made to your new leader?

We all know the startup stress of new work in a new setting among new people. This minister, whom you have just called, is entrusting a season of his or her life to you. He or she has agreed to write the next chapter of your church's ministry life together with you and your congregation, as partners. How will you nurture this new relationship? How will you mutually care for and feed this spiritual bond? Ministers and their families have basic needs for connection to the wider community, for conversation about matters mundane, for recommendations for doctors, dentists, and a good plumber. In the years ahead you may or may not develop a strong bond of personal friendship, but your positivity, helpfulness, and support during this transition matters. You can start by taking an interest, offering hospitality, and being sensitive to needs.

Serving on the Search Team means the minister is not the only one called. You are both the caller and the callee. You will likely be tapped to play some key role in the newly forming next chapter. Think about it: the members of your team are the folks with whom the new pastor has interacted most and is best acquainted, at this point. This often translates into an ongoing commitment to a working relationship. It is critical for you to take the initiative and find ways to offer your witness and support. Pastors sometimes report a sense of being left somewhat abandoned after the official documents are signed on the dotted line. The first six months are critical for saying hello, casting the vision, setting the pace of change, and addressing longstanding log jams. The solidarity of the search team partnering up with the new pastor sends a positive signal internally and to the wider community as well.

Buyer's Remorse

After all is said and done, signed, sealed, and delivered, if your congregation is a typical one, you may silently suffer a few slight twinges of "buyer's remorse." Search teams sometimes scratch their heads and think: What have we gotten ourselves into? Don't be surprised. Cold feet happen. It may interest you to know that the callee may likewise be entertaining thoughts of being elsewhere and otherwise engaged! Ministers have twinges too. (I won't elaborate.)

Please pay attention to this moment. Do not slough off these feelings or dismiss them out of hand. Process them, talk them through, find a way to broach the unbroachable and query the "unqueryable." Ask whether this hesitancy is just a hiccup—is it simply the normal second-guessing? A successful call process can create quite an adrenaline high, and there is a natural let-down period. A search team projects some magical thinking and unreal expectations upon the new leader, and when there are early indications that the leader is all too human, now what? Are the qualms you are quietly confessing within the range of normal? In addition to substantial evidence of the Holy Spirit's leading, there's always a sprinkling of pixie dust spread around the call process. However, not all the rumblings of gut instinct need be attributed to gas. Do you just need to settle into the new normal, or are there legitimate signs of a serious mistake—or a true misunderstanding? Have you all agreed to a call based on a skewed misreading of each other's intentions and expectations? Is it all too late?

Entertaining this inquiry requires fierce courage, because it dances on the precipice of shame, fear, and failure. I know situations in which ministers and congregations broached their trepidations bravely and had "the talk." It was awkward and uncomfortable all around. In some cases, they were able to identify the precipitating factors and missed signals. Sometimes, church factions erupt and politics evoke an early crisis of confidence. Mutual honesty can pave the way for a peaceable parting, if that is appropriate. Of course it's embarrassing, but not as painful as living long term in a situation you both know doesn't have the necessary foundations. If this conversation can be handled with a minimum of judgment and blame, there is a fair possibility of some mutual agreement. Truth be told, I have seen honorable outcomes in which both parties were able to declare: "We have a mismatch based on a mutual misreading, and have agreed to face our situation together." Honorable, indeed.

Sometimes sketching out worst-case scenarios helps put your own qualms in perspective. Most often, if you approach each other with respect, you might be surprised how a little candor laced with humor can help ease initial adjustments. I've watched trust factors deepen exponentially by facing these remorse factors. True, broaching this conversation requires some delicacy, deliberation, and discernment. But if your gut is telling you there is something terribly wrong, stay with the conversation until a measure of resolution emerges. Most often, search teams and clergy work through their initial twinges and proceed to a fruitful season of ministry. Years later, you may laugh together about that time when you all hovered in a moment of suspended animation. Thank God for averted disasters!

Now, I wouldn't want to leave the impression that after all your hard work (discernment *is* hard work!), after buckets of sweat and tears, all the hours invested in conversation are suddenly trashed. Less than 5 percent of calls are "false starts." I have heard just enough horror stories from both sides to feel the need to name this situation as a moment of "transcendental hesitation." If you know in your heart of hearts that something is wrong, and you are just hoping it will all just go away, my advice is: Don't waste these moments of painful openness. Make them count!

Okay, with all the icky stuff in the rearview mirror, let's get on with the party! Your congregation is on the threshold of a new era of life and ministry. Hebrew scripture recounts King David bringing the Ark of the Covenant home to Jerusalem amidst intense rejoicing, expressed in wildly enthusiastic dance before the Lord (2 Sam. 6:14). On this grand occasion, some found reason to critique David's exuberance as unseemly. However, David was unshaken by the naysayers. He did the hard work behind the scenes to recapture the Ark, so his mission was now complete, his spirit undaunted, his joy undiluted, his determination undiminished by differing opinions. He knew very well the dangers, toils, and snares of "bringing it home." He knew the pitfalls and pratfalls better than his detractors would ever dare. All of this aside, it was time for enjoying the goodness of a mission accomplished, so David leaned into the sheer grace of celebration.

I wish more search teams, upon "bringing it home," upon bringing a solid, prayed-through recommendation to the congregation for a final call vote, would dance with all their might before the Lord! Honestly, we Protestants are such a restrained people. Sometimes it seems like the only exercise we get in church is jumping to conclusions! As Garrison Keillor, that master of the Minnesota understatement, might say: "It wouldn't hurt us to praise God with all our might." So, bring it on home, y'all! Bring it on home. Let the joy dance begin! This is a day of new beginnings! Let all that is within us praise the Lord!

Most of the work—the heavy lifting your search team has accomplished—will go unnoticed, unheralded, and under-appreciated. Of course it ought to be otherwise, but the congregation that honors the search team's work is rare. You will be "dismissed with a vote of thanks" in the minutes of the next board meeting. Kind of underwhelming, huh? After all those hours, the endless meetings, the sweat and the prayers…that's it? Yep. You weren't expecting a promotion, were you?

As you probably know, church is not always the best venue for fame and fortune. The folks in the pews are not always good about appreciating work that they never did see.

A little more about this party: Let's gather the search team for a final meeting and celebrate those moments still confidential to the team but well worth remembering. Make it a time of debriefing and declaring the lessons learned.

You were called and commissioned for a specific task in a special season. Now you are being "decommissioned" and returning to "civilian life" in the pews. As you do so, let the words of Psalm 116 ring: "Return, O my soul, to your rest, / for the LORD has dealt bountifully with you."

You have been blessed to be called to serve, blessed in the serving itself, and now blessed in completion of the mission and released to pursue the next stages of God's continuous call on your life.

As you do so, receive this benediction:

"Rest in the grace of God's call through you. Rejoice in the moments when Christ came by your meeting and became your rabbi. Let the quiet goodness of companions in the Spirit bless you often. Your final task is simply this: Take the rest of the day off to 'magnify the Lord and let us exalt God's name together.'"

Good *work,* team! Let the lessons and the laughter linger!

DEVOTIONAL REFLECTIONS

Biblical images for use as search
team meditations

1. Looking on the heart—1 Samuel 16:7.

    "...but the LORD looks on the heart."

    Outward appearances are important, but not always the deciding factor. How do you measure inner devotion, attitudes, and mental habits? Are you looking for a superhero?

2. Peaceable words of agreement—Acts 15:28

    "For it has seemed good to the Holy Spirit and to us..."

    Notice the order? First the selection seemed good to the Spirit, and then us. How would you go about knowing that?

3. Elijah's mantle—2 Kings 2:9–18

    "...a double share of your spirit."

    Sometimes a candidate seems almost anointed, evoking the memory of beloved leaders. How would you go about confirming such an impression?

4. Esther's timely call—Esther 4:14

    "Perhaps you have come...for just such a time as this."

    Timing is everything. The right person at the right time for the right purpose might be a sign of God's kairos timing at work.

5. Daniel's vision-quest—Daniel 10:7–14

    "Stand on your feet, for I have now been sent to you."

    Often a search team seeks the convergence of vision with future mission. Would we know a vision if it stared at us from the face of an angel? (or a candidate?)

6. Elijah's earthquake call 1 Kings 19:7

    "Get up and eat, otherwise the journey will be too much for you..."

    Sustenance for the search comes from the hand of God, who provides what is needed.

7. Angels of the seven churches—Revelation 3:8a,13

    "Listen to what the Spirit is saying to the churches."

    Are we so preoccupied with our search process that we are ignoring the larger Word?

8. Discernment image: chaff in wind—Psalm 1:4

    "tossing wheat in air, trusting grain to gravity; chaff to blow away"

One form of surrender might be trusting our decision to the wind of the Spirit.

9. Circumstantial guidance for God's servant—Genesis 24:27

   "As for me, the LORD has led me on the way…"

   So much of ministry is showing up and being attentive as guidance appears.

10. Calls arising out of vision—Acts 10:1–10; 16:6–10

    " but the Spirit forbid- did not allow- Come over to Macedonia and help us"

    Much as we imagine the search process as logical, mercy and mystery remain.

Twenty Questions Search Teams Ask Themselves

1. With our minister in place for so long, much of our congregational life is just taken for granted. How will we reassume and reassert institutional memory during this transition?

2. Grieving will likely take longer than we think. How will we shepherd the congregation through the transitional process, from "previous pastor zone" to the "neutral zone" and finally into the "new pastor zone"?

3. Alliances that gel around staff personalities must be sifted and sorted in the interim. While appreciating past loyalties, how do we help reset staff relationships? What might help untangle this a bit?

4. The official Search and Call process seems complicated, even labyrinthian. We will need some schooling on the rules. How will we learn the system, clarify appropriate protocols, and also keep our process moving forward with all due deliberate haste?

5. "Courting" a senior minister is a lost art. What's our learning curve? If we are a bit out of practice, how will we get in practice?

6. Assuming that within the official call system there is a pool of candidates who are potential matches, how can we do our homework on these churches? Are there tools available for research? How do we perform due diligence and demonstrate our initiative, resourcefulness, connection, and competence?

7. How will we treat a candidate's family? However much of an adventure the search conversation may be for a candidate, the process may look a little different to his or her family. How will we assist them in evaluating the potential of this call from their perspective, needs, and interests?

8. Are we personally prepared to articulate our mission, vision, and values, as well as future dreams? Are we each clear about our personal stake in this congregation?

9. As we develop a detailed profile of the kind of leader we seek, how would we describe the DNA of our church? What would definitely *not* work? Why is that?

10. Are we prepared to "sell" the community? Are we knowledgeable enough to showcase local advantages and demonstrate them during the candidate's brief visit?

11. Are we staying two jumps ahead in the process, structuring the initial approach as well as scripting the first visit (candidate only? family too?) What tone do we want to strike? Does the way we've set up the visit schedule and itinerary resonate with the impression we hope to convey? Check the overall flow.

12. How will we get a window into this leader's soul and offer him or her a window into our church's heart and soul? Without this touch, how can we discern a match? Won't this be time-consuming? How might we create some space for mutual discernment?

13. What is our agreed-upon understanding of team confidentiality? How have we decided to manage violations of confidentiality?

14. Do we know specifically what a minister's family is looking for in this move? What are the deliverables and what are the dreams?

15. How are we paying attention to the little things that make for thoughtful hospitality? Do we know the deal-breakers/makers for this family? What is the spouse's (or significant other's) line of work? Will he or she continue a career or advance educational goals? How is the family planning to dovetail this move vocationally? How might the congregation assist with introductions and connections?

16. Have we structured a job description with full discussion and disclosure of expectations around

the sensitive areas? Who's the staff team leader?

17. Talking about compensation requires a common language and some grounding principles. (discussed under Points of Agreement on pages 66–70) Have we researched comparable positions in the local community? Have we factored in special needs and conditions? What family concerns impinge or enhance? Will there be built-in incentives to grow professionally and produce effective results? How will we agree to evaluate performance to award such incentives? Will this pastor need to consider a move in five years just to get the kind of raises that keep pace with economic factors and family needs? We learn a lot about a candidate's money mindset (and our own) in this kind of negotiation. Are all the assumptions on the table?

18. How will the team structure and manage the presentation of the final candidate and the terms of call to the board and congregation? Agree on the protocols and procedures ahead of time. Will there be a letter of call issued? Will the details of call and compensation be held in confidence? If so, for how long? Why or why not?

19. What will be the search team's role in the transition process? Will we become part of a transition team? What will the welcoming committee look like? How do we see the interim minister assisting transitional efforts?

20. How is the congregation's relationship to former pastors understood, articulated, and practiced? Who will monitor this mutual understanding? What would an ideal relational connection look like? What in our mind would constitute a violation or create a potential problem for the new minister?

BONUS QUESTION: How will you communicate your process, progress, and selection to the congregation at large? What if your team ends in a split vote with some accommodation for reservations? In other words, what constitutes a call? Will you just "know one when you see one"? What are your entry plans for this new chapter of mission and ministry? Will you do a debrief of the team's work and thank God for this extraordinary honor?

....

Appreciation to Karol Priester of Sun City Christian Church, whose technical help and prayerful spirit proved invaluable in finalizing the manuscript.

ADDITIONAL RESOURCES

Bridges, William, "Managing Transitions," Perseus Books, 1991. Helpful overview of process; easily adaptable to church life.

Oswald, Roy, "Running through the Thistles: Terminating a Ministerial Relationship with a Parish," Alban Institute, 2011. An old standby full of practicable suggestions.

Steinke, Peter, "Congregational Leadership in Anxious Times: Being Calm and Courageous No Matter What," Rowman/Littlefield, 2006. Insightful application of family systems theory as diagnostic tool. .

Straub, Gary, "Your Calling as an Elder," Chalice Press, 1995. Guidance on spiritual leadership.

Woolever, Cynthia, and Deborah Bruce, "Leadership that Fits Your Church: What Kind of Pastor for What Kind of Congregation," Chalice Press, 2012. Solid updated research; excellent section on pastor/congregation match.

ABOUT THE AUTHOR
Gary Straub

Dr. Straub has served congregations in Kentucky and Tennessee, and for the last decade has served as an intentional Interim Minister in a variety of Disciples congregations including Woodmont Christian Church in Nashville, Tennessee; Riverside Christian Church in Jacksonville, Florida; First Christian Church in Jeffersonville, Indiana; Zionsville Christian Church in Zionsville, Indiana, Northwood Christian Church in Indianapolis, and Saguaro Christian Church in Tucson, Arizona. In between interims he has also served as a consultant and part-time staff person at Beargrass Christian Church and Middletown Christian Church in Louisville, Kentucky. In the wider church, he has chaired the boards of Church Extension and Homeland Ministries in the Christian Church (Disciples of Christ).

Straub's education includes a bachelor's degree from Ozark Bible College, master's and doctorate degrees from Vanderbilt Divinity School, a Master of Theology from Princeton Theological Seminary, coaching certification, and spiritual direction training with Shalem Institute.

Straub's other books from Chalice Press are *Your Calling as an Elder, Your Calling as a Deacon,* and *Your Calling as a Leader.*

He is a frequent workshop leader around questions of spiritual leadership development.

Currently Straub is an active consultant/mentor with Bethany Fellows (bethanyfellows.org), which serves congregations by helping young pastors transition from seminary to sustained congregational ministry with a strong and healthy sense of pastoral identity. He helps coordinate an informal network that shares resources for prayerful, practical solutions. Reach Gary at gary@bethanyfellows.org.

CPSIA information can be obtained
at www.ICGtesting.com
Printed in the USA
LVHW081515080221
678722LV00018B/4068